A Pocket of Time

the poetic childhood of elizabeth bishop

Words by **RITA WILSON**

Art by **EMMA FITZGERALD**

NIMBUS
PUBLISHING LTD
— NIMBUS.CA —

This is for the children:
Rose, a poet rising,
Rilka and Amos, just beginning,
and always, for Sheilah, Daniel, Matthew, and Catherine.
–RW

To the caretakers of the EB House, most especially Sandra Barry.
–EF

Words © 2019, Rita Wilson
Artwork © 2019, Emma FitzGerald

Editor: Whitney Moran
Cover design: Emma FitzGerald
Interior design: Heather Bryan
Photographs of Bishop and family courtesy of Acadia University Archives, Vaughan Memorial Library, Acadia University, Wolfville, Nova Scotia, Canada.

Library and Archives Canada Cataloguing in Publication

Title: A pocket of time : the poetic childhood of Elizabeth Bishop / words by Rita Wilson art by Emma FitzGerald.
Names: Wilson, Rita, 1947- author. | FitzGerald, Emma, 1982- illustrator.
Identifiers: Canadiana 20190169303 | ISBN 9781771088091 (hardcover)
Subjects: LCSH: Bishop, Elizabeth, 1911-1979—Childhood and youth.
Classification: LCC PS3503.I785 Z935 2019 | DDC 811/.54—dc23

Nimbus Publishing acknowledges the financial support for its publishing activities from the Government of Canada, the Canada Council for the Arts, and from the Province of Nova Scotia We are pleased to work in partnership with the Province of Nova Scotia to develop and promote our creative industries for the benefit of all Nova Scotians.

Introduction

A little girl lies sick in bed with a rattly chest. A doctor, leaning over, asks her to stick out her tongue. He makes a rhyme, "Lambs say baaa, can you say aaah?" She laughs in delight.

That same girl, healthy again, is getting ready for church. Her grandmother polishes her Sunday shoes, using gasoline to clean the white tops and Vaseline for the patent leather bottoms. The girl marches around all day, chanting, *Vaseline/gasoline, Vaseline/gasoline*. Years later she said, *It may not have been a poem, but it was my first rhyme.*

That girl, Elizabeth Bishop, grew up to become a famous poet.

She was born in Worcester, Massachusetts, in 1911 to William and Gertrude Bishop. Her father died when she was a baby and, after his death, she spent time in the small town of Great Village, Nova Scotia, where her mother's parents—Gammie and Pa to Elizabeth—lived in a white clapboard house.

It was at Gammie and Pa's that Elizabeth remembered learning to walk, to read, to write, to sing hymns, and to catch bumblebees in foxglove flowers. It's where she first went to school and, when she was five, it's where her mother left for the Nova Scotia Hospital (a mental hospital also known as Mount Hope) from which she never returned. And it is at Gammie and Pa's that this story takes place.

Turn the page and you will enter Elizabeth's Great Village world. My words will take you, along with Elizabeth, through each room of Gammie and Pa's house and out into the town. This book has been inspired by Elizabeth's own writing, the poems and stories she wrote about that piece of her childhood when she lived in Great Village with Gammie and Pa. Her own words (which you will see in *italics*, in quotation marks, in stamps, and further notated in the back of this book) will tell you what she played, what she learned, what she noticed. They will also tell you what confused her, what excited her, and what she wondered about.

Meet this girl who fell in love with words, and who used her childhood memories to recreate her Great Village world for each of us.

Walk up the path on the side of the house, past the landmark elm, past the foxgloves, the cosmos, the Johnny-jump-ups.

Elizabeth sits on the back steps, peeling the paper off her slate pencil, holding a slate on her lap. Gammie has taught her to write her name, the names of the people in her family, of their dog and cats. She notices the letters she makes have "different expressions"; sometimes the capital E and B in her name look almost sad, but other times...

they turned fat and cheerful, almost with roses in their cheeks.

E lizabeth is singing as she walks to the horse trough, but her song stops partway through. For a long time, she would only sing the alphabet to the letter G, satisfied with the shape of that short tune. Until someone laughed at her and, quickly, she decided to go all the way to Z.

She loves to wash her slate in the watering trough, watching the letters and words disappear…

It dried like clouds.

ammie must have called to Elizabeth; she's in the kitchen tasting something on a wooden spoon—potato mash for tomorrow's bread! Elizabeth thinks that it tastes wonderful, but wrong.

She had noticed Gammie crying while stirring the mash and wonders if it's the taste of her tears. She kisses Gammie and tastes tears on her cheek.

With crayons the child draws...a man with buttons like tears

alk into the pantry off the kitchen. Long and narrow, it stores all kinds of things in its twenty-seven drawers and cupboards. Elizabeth is on the floor, opening the door to her shelf.

There are old books and toys and a strawberry basket inside. In the basket are the marbles she's been searching for. The biggest, the one Elizabeth thinks the most beautiful, is shiny and pink, made of crockery, like the cup she drinks tea with milk from in the morning. When she picks it up, it moves her…

almost to tears to look at it.

It's suppertime, and everyone is around the dining room table. Inside a cage hanging from a hook in the ceiling, a canary nibbles chickweed that Gammie sent Elizabeth across the road to pick. Earlier, you would have heard Pa saying grace, always the same way. Elizabeth thinks that when he says, "We have *reasons* to thank Thee," he's actually saying, We have *raisins* to thank Thee.

Supper is finished. The lamp has yet to be lit. The day is moving from dusk to dark. Elizabeth looks at the windowpanes and notices the reflections there. She sees herself, she sees her grandmother, and wonders: where were they before?

Here we all were,
at last doubly together.

Not quite bedtime, they've gathered in the sitting room. Pa's in his Morris chair reading the newspaper, Nanny the cat on his lap. Aunt Mary's reading *Maclean's* magazine. Elizabeth is on the floor, colouring.

There are books on the table by Pa's chair. Sometimes he reads poetry out loud. Robbie Burns is a favourite, and Pa reads his poems with a bit of a Scottish accent:

"O my Luve's like a red, red rose

That's newly sprung in June;

O my Luve's like the melodie

That's sweetly play'd in tune."

Gammie is tatting lace, with her one good eye. Her glass eye sometimes looks off at an angle, while her real eye looks right at you. Both eyes are almost the same colour blue, but to Elizabeth, the glass eye…

made her especially vulnerable and precious

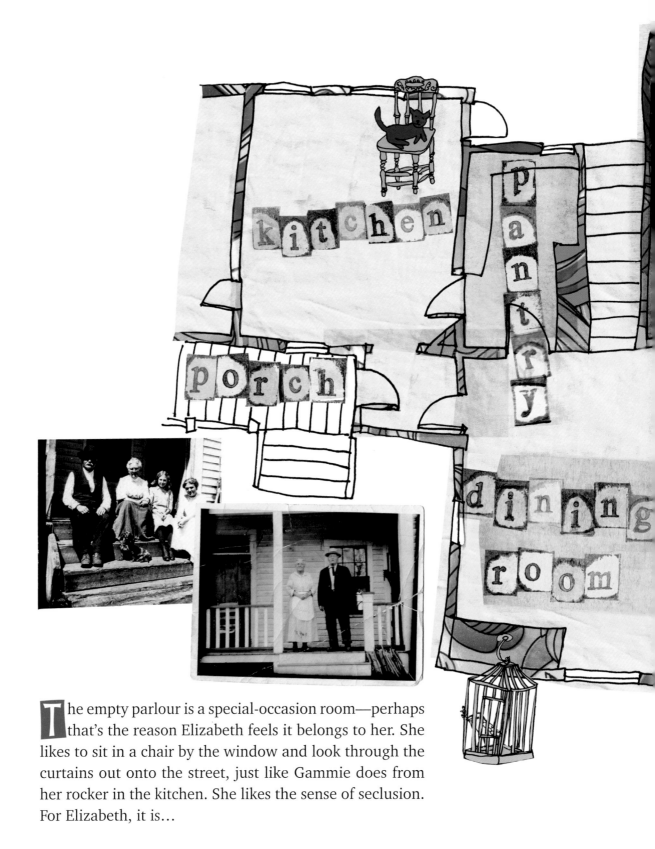

kitchen

pantry

porch

dining room

The empty parlour is a special-occasion room—perhaps that's the reason Elizabeth feels it belongs to her. She likes to sit in a chair by the window and look through the curtains out onto the street, just like Gammie does from her rocker in the kitchen. She likes the sense of seclusion. For Elizabeth, it is…

the one place where I could think...as from a distance....

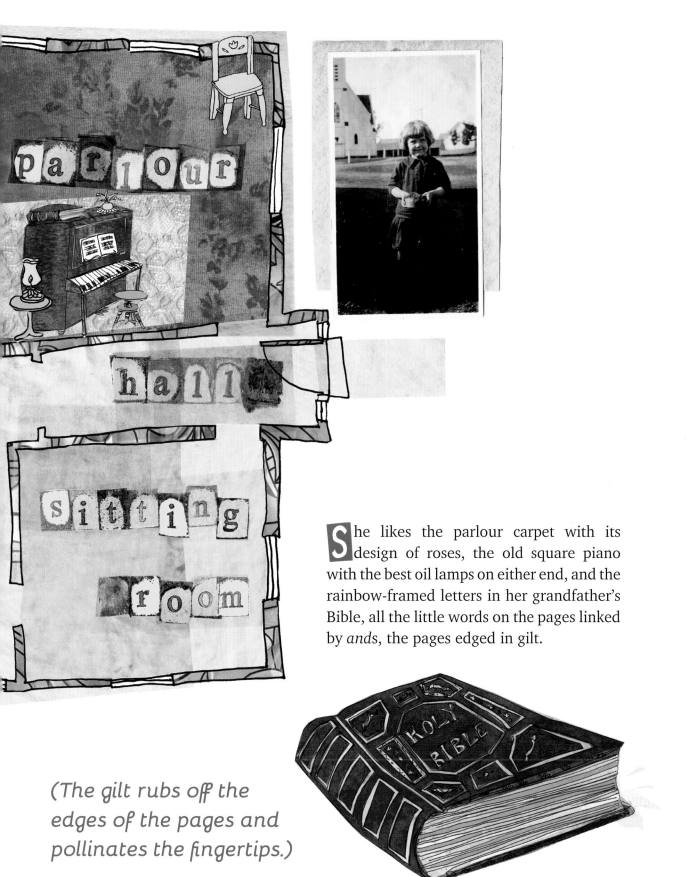

parlour

hall

sitting

room

She likes the parlour carpet with its design of roses, the old square piano with the best oil lamps on either end, and the rainbow-framed letters in her grandfather's Bible, all the little words on the pages linked by *and*s, the pages edged in gilt.

(The gilt rubs off the edges of the pages and pollinates the fingertips.)

HOLY BIBLE

When it's time for bed, Pa holds an oil lamp as Elizabeth climbs the ladder-like stairs to her room. Gammie calls from the sitting room to Elizabeth to say her prayers. After Pa puts her to bed, he puts the lamp, turned low, on the sewing machine table in the hall and leaves her door ajar. He doesn't want Elizabeth to be afraid of the dark—even though she tells him that she's not.

Elizabeth loves her kind and jokey grandfather. He's her favourite relative.

How far north are you by now?

—But I'm almost close enough to see you:

under the North Star.

Portaupique Landing
Pa Bulmer

Picnic 1918

Elizabeth sleeps in the "little" room, right next to her Aunt Mary's. It is special because it has a skylight over the bed. She was sick a lot last winter with bronchitis. To fill the time, Gammie let her play with the button basket, so big and full it must have weighed ten pounds…

filled with everything from the metal snaps for men's overalls to a set of large cut-steel buttons

…and the scrap bag, filled with familiar pieces of fabric: one from Pa's shirt, another from someone else's pants. There's even a scrap from the housedress Gammie's wearing right now.

Better yet is the crazy quilt Gammie made, every piece of silk or velvet telling a tale about a person in the village. Gammie had collected them all from friends over the years, getting each friend to write their name in pencil on their piece. Then she stitched their names in chains of coloured silk thread.

Best of all is when Gammie comes at the end of the day. The dark comes early, and Gammie wraps Elizabeth in a blanket and places her on her lap. In the rocking chair they rock back and forth, back and forth. Gammie sings hymns to her.

(I'm full of hymns by the way—...and I often catch echoes from them in my own poems).

The front bedroom, with slanted ceilings and striped wallpaper, is the largest. Out the window are elm trees, lilac bushes, and a grey roof patched with moss that belongs to the blacksmith shop next door.

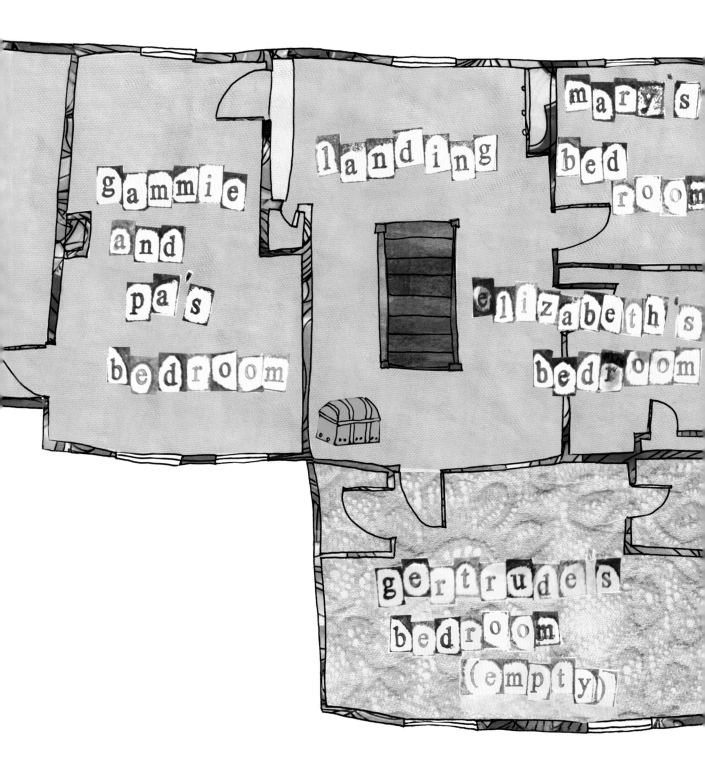

At the end of the hall and right next to Elizabeth's is Gertrude, her mother's room….

My ears would listen listen…
Often nothing could be heard.

There was a time when her mother came and went, to and from Great Village. Then she was gone.

Now the front bedroom is empty.

As she lays in her bed in the soft light from the hallway, Elizabeth can hear almost every word that Gammie and Pa speak from their bedroom across the hall. She is a little pitcher with big ears, listening for their stories and secrets in the night.

Talking the way they talked

in the old featherbed

peacefully, on and on

There are mornings when Elizabeth can't bear to wait for her Aunt Mary (who spends a lot of time upstairs braiding her hair, tying and retying the bow on her middy blouse) to leave for school. She finds her slate and the rag to wash it, fills the medicine bottle with water, leans over to pat Betsy, their dachshund, goodbye, kisses Gammie (making her promise not to die before she comes home), and heads out on her own.

Waving to Nate in the blacksmith shop, Elizabeth walks onto the one-lane metal bridge that rumbles when horses and wagons drive over, and stands by the railing. She loves to stare at the river rushing by, watching for the "too-smart-to-get-caught" trout as they swim past a long sunk rusting fender.

Once in a while, the river gives an unexpected gurgle. "Slp," it says...

Then, Elizabeth hears the first bell and hurries on.

The school is up ahead, tall and white, a dark red roof, a cupola on top. Elizabeth walks quickly, anxious to get there before the second bell rings. Inside are rows of desks bolted to the floor. Two maps, hanging from the wall, fascinate Elizabeth.

I was so taken with the pull-down maps that I wanted to... touch all the countries and provinces with my own hands.

One great room holds primary to grade four. The teacher, Georgie Morash, listens to the children reading, pointer in hand. Elizabeth loves the older children's stories, they're much more interesting than the short ones she's memorized in her own small brown primer. She's coloured many of the pictures in the book, and written her name over and over in her…

embryonic handwriting.

On her way home, Elizabeth hears the sounds of the blacksmith shop.

Clang.

Clang.

Nate's song: the creak of the bellows, the hammering of a horseshoe into place.

Elizabeth stops and calls out,

Make me a ring, Nate!

Nate hands her something so quickly it's still hot, and it's hers! It is…

blue and shiny. The horseshoe nail has a flat oblong head, pressing hot against my knuckle.

Gammie's waiting on the porch and, after admiring Elizabeth's ring, hands her a package to take to the post office.

Elizabeth walks by the blacksmith shop, pretending she doesn't hear Nate's greeting, and then over the bridge, past Mealy's shop, to the tilting-over post office.

She stands at the outside window while Mr. Johnson, the postmaster, reaches for the package she is tightly grasping.

Every Monday, Gammie fills a box with treats—fruit and cake, wild strawberry jam, a handkerchief with a tatted edge, books—for Elizabeth's mother in the mental hospital. Every Monday, Elizabeth carries that package to the post office, holding it against her body to hide the address.

The address of the sanatorium is in my grandmother's handwriting.... It will never come off.

While she's there, she goes inside to see if there's mail in their box, number twenty-one.

Sometimes there are postcards; today is one of those times. Often they come from Boston, from those other grandparents who send things through the mail. Elizabeth has noticed a lot of things in the village are from Boston. She knows that she, too, once lived there.

But I remembered only being here....

Hurrying home, Elizabeth gives Gammie the postcard, knowing it's time to get Nelly, their Jersey cow, from Chisholm's pasture. It's her favourite chore,

marching through the village with a big stick, directing her.

When Elizabeth gets up the hill to the pasture, she loves to look out over the entire village.

There are the tops of all the elm trees in the village and there, beyond them, the long green marshes, so fresh, so salt.

She finds Nelly, with her drool like glass strings and her shiny blue nose, gives her hipbone a whack with the stick, and heads down the hill. They walk past the MacLachlan farm, past the Presbyterian manse, avoiding Miss Spencer's lilac bush, as they make their way home.

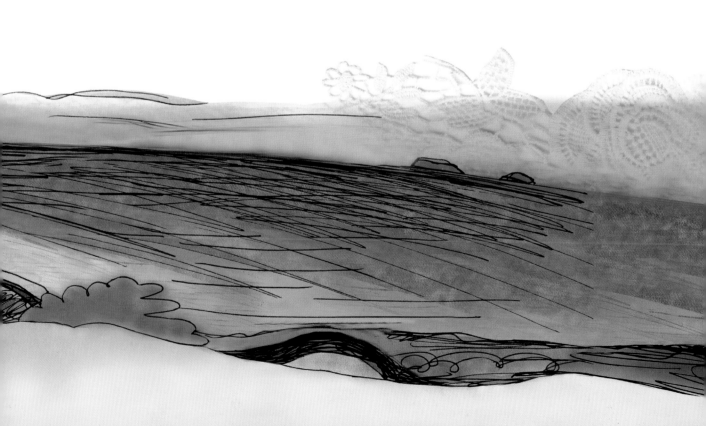

It's almost suppertime when Elizabeth gets home, and Gammie says it's time to get "fixed up." She lets Elizabeth brush her silver hair, full of combs of matching silver-coloured celluloid. Elizabeth stands on the rungs of the rocking chair, swaying and brushing, pretending…

to play a tune…before we stick them in, so my grandmother's hair is full of music….

Pa comes in to wash up, and while he's drying his hands Gammie shows him the postcard. He shakes his head, murmuring, "oh pshaw," and Gammie repeats her familiar refrain,

Nobody knows, nobody knows.

Elizabeth wonders what message that postcard contains, and asks,

"What do you know, Gammie, that we don't know?..."

There are, always, so many things to wonder about.

Although there are more, these are all the memories I want to keep on remembering....

Postscript

When Elizabeth was six, her father's parents, those other grandparents who had been no more than postcards and packages from Boston, decided that she should live with them in their big house in Worcester, Massachusetts. They came to Great Village and took Elizabeth away with them on the train. She had not been asked, and she would not have agreed.

Little did she know, it was the beginning of a life filled with journeys—some happy, some sad—that took her many places in the world. She came back to Great Village each summer for the next ten years, while Gammie and Pa were still alive.

Thirty-five years later, living far away in Brazil, Elizabeth used these Great Village memories to write some of her most famous poems and stories. She said, "It's funny to come to Brazil to experience total recall about Nova Scotia— geography must be more mysterious than we realize, even."

One of those poems, "A Short, Slow Life," is about that time in Great Village, before she was taken away. It begins,

We lived in a pocket of time.
It was close. It was warm.

That first line not only became the title of this book, it also became my inspiration to learn about that Great Village time, through Bishop's own work. Her words painted a picture that was filled with details that slid into poetry, about a child's life, Elizabeth's own life with Gammie and Pa, until she was forced to move away.

All these things that happened in Elizabeth's childhood put home, and the search for home, at the heart of her life and her writing.

Acknowledgements

First, thanks to Sandra Barry, who opened the door to Bishop, literally, and has held it open ever since, with her generosity, her passion, and her deep knowledge.

To the Elizabeth Bishop Society, for nurturing and celebrating the Great Village connection; to Joy Laking and Laurie Gunn for keeping the house open.

My gratitude to the spirit of Sheree Fitch, who read this manuscript early and with enthusiasm, then mapped a path of possibility to publication.

Thanks to Nimbus Publishing, especially Whitney Moran, for her skilled editing, making the drastic seem possible.

To Emma FitzGerald, a passionate Bishopite, who makes pictures out of poems.

To my writing group, who listened and kept me at it.

To all the friends and family who encouraged, especially the new branches: Dani, Donna, and Kerry.

For all the word-loving children: my own, those I taught, and their children.

And, to Elizabeth Bishop's memory.

–RW

Bibliography

Conversations with Elizabeth Bishop, ed. George Monteiro, University Press of Mississippi, 1996.

Elizabeth Bishop, *The Collected Prose*, ed. Robert Giroux, Farrar, Straus, Giroux, 1984.

Elizabeth Bishop, *The Complete Poems 1927-1979*, Farrar, Straus, Giroux, 1979.

Elizabeth Bishop, *Edgar Allan Poe & The Juke-Box*, edited and annotated by Alice Quinn, Farrar, Straus, Giroux, 2006.

Elizabeth Bishop, *Poems, Prose and Letters, ed. Lloyd Schwartz and Robert Giroux, No. 180 Library of America Series*, 2008.

"*Reminiscences of Great Village*," unpublished manuscript, Vassar College Special Collections. It is part of the Elizabeth Bishop Papers. Series V, Folder 54.10.

References by Page Number:

3   "It may not have been a poem, but it was my first rhyme." (*Conversations with EB*, p. 71)

4   "different expressions" ("Primer Class," *The Collected Prose*, p. 12)

4–5 "they turned fat and cheerful, almost with roses in their cheeks"; "it dried like clouds" ("Primer Class," *The Collected Prose*, p. 12)

6   "With crayons the child draws…a man with buttons like tears" ("Sestina," *The Collected Poems*, p. 123)

7   "almost to tears to look at it" ("Gwendolyn," *The Collected Prose*, p. 224)

8   "Here we all were, at last doubly together." ("Reminiscences of Great Village," *The Collected Prose*, p. 6)

11   "made her especially vulnerable and precious" ("Primer Class," *The Collected Prose*, p. 6)

12   "the one place where I could think…as from a distance…." (*Poems, Prose and Letters*, p. 707)

13   "(*The gilt rubs off the edges/of the pages and pollinates the fingertips.*)" ("Over 2,000 Illustrations and a Complete Concordance," *The Complete Poems*, p. 56)

15   "How far north are you by now?…" ("For Grandfather," *The Collected Poems*, p. 154)

16   "filled with everything from the metal snaps for men's overalls to a set of large cut-steel buttons" ("Gwendolyn," *The Collected Prose*, p. 214)

17   "(I'm full of hymns by the way - . . . and I often catch echoes from them in my poems." ("Reminisces of Great Village," *The Collected Prose*, p. 215)

19   "My ears would listen listen…Often nothing could be heard" ; "Now the front bedroom is empty." ("In the Village," *The Collected Prose*, p. 271)

21   "Talking the way they talked/in the old featherbed/peacefully, on and on." ("The Moose," *The Complete Poems*, p. 172)

23   "Once in a while, the river gives an unexpected gurgle. "Slp," it says…" ("In the Village," *The Collected Prose*, p. 274)

24   "I was so taken with the pull-down maps that I wanted to…touch all the countries and provinces with my own hands." ("Primer Class," *The Collected Prose*, p. 10)

25   "embryonic handwriting" (*Elizabeth Bishop: Poems, Prose and Letters*, p. 707)

26–27 *Clang. Clang.*"; "Make me a ring, Nate!"; "blue and shiny. The horseshoe nail has a flat oblong head, pressing hot against my knuckle." ("In the Village," *The Collected Prose*, pp. 252; 257)

29   "The address of the sanatorium is in my grandmother's handwriting…. It will never come off." ("In the Village," *The Collected Prose*, p. 272)

30   "But I remembered only being here…" ("In the Village," *The Collected Prose*, p. 254)

31   "marching through the village with a big stick, directing her." ("In the Village," *The Collected Prose*, p. 260)

32   "There are the tops of all the elm trees in the village and there, beyond them, the long green marshes, so fresh, so salt." ("In the Village," *The Collected Prose*, p. 264)

34   "to play a tune…before we stick them in, so my grandmother's hair is full of music" ("In the Village," *The Collected Prose*, p. 260)

36   "What do you know, Gammie, that we don't know?" ("Memories of Uncle Neddy," *The Collected Prose*, pp. 241-2); "Although there are more, these are all the memories I want to keep on remembering." ("Memories of Uncle Neddy," *The Collected Prose*, p. 249)

37   "We lived in a pocket of time…." ("A Short, Slow Life," *Elizabeth Bishop, Edgar Allan Poe & The Juke Box*, p. 234)